MW00650548

REDISCOVERING THE LOST ART OF
FRIENDSHIP

A Saddleback Church Small Group Study

REDISCOVERING THE LOST ART OF FRIENDSHIP
A Saddleback Church Small Group Study

Copyright © 2023 by Saddleback Church

All rights reserved. No part of this book may be reproduced, stored in a retrieval system, or transmitted in any form without the publisher's written permission.

 SADDLEBACK CHURCH

Published by Saddleback Valley Community Church
1 Saddleback Parkway
Lake Forest, CA 92630
saddleback.com

ISBN: 978-1-959074-21-2

Editors: Heather Cova, Rob Jacobs, Linda Tokar, Jason Wieland, and Jacob Wilson

---

Scripture quotations noted CEV are from the CONTEMPORARY ENGLISH VERSION. Copyright © 1991, 1992, 1995 by American Bible Society. Used by permission.

Scripture quotations noted ESV are from the Holy Bible, ENGLISH STANDARD VERSION®. Copyright © 2001 by Crossway, a publishing ministry of Good News Publishers. Used by permission. All rights reserved.

Scripture quotations noted GW are from GOD'S WORD®. Copyright © 1995, 2003, 2013, 2014, 2019, 2020 by God's Word to the Nations Mission Society. Used by permission.

Scripture quotations noted HCSB are from the HOLMAN CHRISTIAN STUDY BIBLE®. Copyright © 1999, 2000, 2002, 2003, 2009 by Holman Bible Publishers. Used by permission. Holman Christian Standard Bible®, Holman CSB®, and HCSB® are federally registered trademarks of Holman Bible Publishers.

Scripture quotations noted NASB95 are from the NEW AMERICAN STANDARD BIBLE®, Copyright © 1960, 1971, 1977, 1995 by The Lockman Foundation. Used by permission. All rights reserved. *lockman.org*

Scripture quotations noted NCV are from the NEW CENTURY VERSION®. Copyright © 2005 by Thomas Nelson. Used by permission. All rights reserved.

Scripture quotations noted NET are from THE NET BIBLE® *netbible.com*, Copyright © 1996, 2019 used with permission from Biblical Studies Press, L.L.C. All rights reserved.

Scripture quotations noted NIV are from the Holy Bible, NEW INTERNATIONAL VERSION®, NIV®. Copyright © 1973, 1978, 1984, 2011 by Biblica, Inc.® Used by permission. All rights reserved worldwide.

Scripture quotations noted NLT are from the NEW LIVING TRANSLATION® (NLT). Copyright © 1996, 2004, 2015 by Tyndale House Foundation. Used by permission of Tyndale House Publishers Inc., Carol Stream, Illinois 60188. All rights reserved.

Scripture quotations noted NRSV are from the NEW REVISED STANDARD VERSION BIBLE. Copyright © 1989 by the Division of Christian Education of the National Council of the Churches of Christ in the U.S.A. Used by permission. All rights reserved.

Scripture quotations noted VOICE are from The Voice™. Copyright © 2008 by Ecclesia Bible Society. Used by permission. All rights reserved.

Contents

Letter from Pastor Andy Wood *4*

Understanding Your Study Guide *6*

How to Use This Curriculum *9*

Week 1: INITIATE *14*
Follow Jesus' Approach

Week 2: INVEST *26*
Build a Strong Foundation

Week 3: ENRICH *52*
Experience God's Beautiful and Diverse Family

Week 4: STRENGTHEN *76*
Cultivate Openness and Honesty

Week 5: DISCERN *96*
Select the Right Friends

Small Group Resources *121*
Helps for Hosts *122*
Frequently Asked Questions *128*
Small Group Guidelines *130*
Circles of Life *132*
Prayer and Praise Report *133*
Small Group Calendar *134*

Additional Resources *135*

Small Group Roster *139*

Letter from Pastor Andy Wood

Dear Friend,

Friendships have always been a part of God's original design. After God created Adam in Genesis 2:18 NASB95, he said, *"It is not good for the man to be alone. I will make a helper suitable for him."* We were made and formed by God to be in relationship with him, and with each other. It's how he designed us.

You already know this—you know how much better life is when you have friends who love you and walk through life with you. We weren't meant to do life alone. But as technology is growing, and we're building more relationships online, there's a relational deficit in our culture. And for many of us it may feel like we're more surrounded by people than we've ever been, yet more isolated than we've ever been.

This study talks practically about how to build friendships that withstand the test of time. We need people who rejoice when we rejoice, weep when we weep, and are with us through the good times and the hard times. By following Jesus' example, and the example of other people we see in Scripture, we'll build a roadmap of the best way to build these kinds of friendships.

In a world plagued by loneliness and disconnection, there is an urgent need for genuine and lasting friendships. As Christians, we have the opportunity to learn from the greatest friend of all time: Jesus himself.

I'm so excited to start this journey together!

Pastor Andy Wood
Lead Pastor
Saddleback Church

Understanding Your Study Guide

Here is a brief explanation of the features of this study guide.

GAME PLAN

Each week's topic begins with an agenda to help you navigate the content for that week. The organization and content pieces may change from week to week or you might be asked to bring something to your small group meeting for that week's **GROUP ACTIVITY**. The **GAME PLAN** section for that week will ensure you are prepared and on track for each and every week.

INTRODUCTION

Each week features a written **INTRODUCTION**. Be sure to read the **INTRODUCTION** for Week 1 during your small group meeting. The **INTRODUCTION** section for the remaining weeks is meant to be read on your own prior to your next meeting.

REDISCOVERING THE LOST ART OF FRIENDSHIP PODCAST

A limited-series podcast produced by Saddleback Church has been created to accompany this study. Each week has a brief explanation of the podcast episode for that week and a link to listen to the episode.

DAILY BIBLE READING

Except for Week 1, each week features a **DAILY BIBLE READING** plan for that week (five days). Each day has the passage(s) for that day, along with some reflective questions or exercises. Use the space in these sections to write out your thoughts to these questions.

Week 1 has a single Bible passage to be read together during your small group time.

DISCUSSION QUESTIONS

Two to three questions are presented for you to talk about during your small group time. Please don't feel pressured to discuss every single question. There is no reason to rush through the answers. Give everyone ample opportunity to share their thoughts. If you don't get through all of the **DISCUSSION QUESTIONS**, that's okay.

GROUP ACTIVITY

Since this study is about building strong friendships, the primary piece of this study is the **GROUP ACTIVITY**. You are given an activity to do together during your small group time each week. Detailed instructions are provided for each activity.

PRAYER DIRECTION

Spend some time in prayer at the end of each
session. Use the brief prompts to help guide your
prayer times.

ONE LAST THING

Close your group each week by following the
directions in this section. It gives information
that is important for your next group meeting.

SMALL GROUP RESOURCES

There are additional small group resources,
such as **SMALL GROUP GUIDELINES, HELPS
FOR HOSTS**, and **PRAYER AND PRAISE
REPORT**, in the back of this study guide.

How to Use This Curriculum

Follow the instructions below to navigate this study successfully.

Week 1

Your Week 1 small group meeting will follow a different format than the other weeks.

- Open your group meeting by reading the Week 1 **GAME PLAN**.

- Read the **INTRODUCTION** to Week 1 and the following **DAILY BIBLE READING** together.

- As a group, talk through the **DISCUSSION QUESTIONS**, do the **GROUP ACTIVITY**, and the **ONE LAST THING**, which will prepare your group for the next week.

- Close your group time by following the **PRAYER DIRECTION** and looking at the following week's **GAME PLAN** together.

- Sometime after your first group meeting, listen to Episode 1 of the *Rediscovering the Lost Art of Friendship Podcast.*

Weeks 2 through 5

Weeks 2 through 5 have a different format to be followed. Some portions of each week's content will need to be completed before the next meeting.

- Read the **INTRODUCTION** each week on your own.

- Read the **DAILY BIBLE READING** over the five days between your group meetings. Engage with the accompanying reflection questions each day.

- During the week, listen to the *Rediscovering the Lost Art of Friendship Podcast.*

- During your group meeting, talk through the **DISCUSSION QUESTIONS** and do the **GROUP ACTIVITY** together.

- To close your group time, follow the **PRAYER DIRECTION** and the **ONE LAST THING**, which will prepare your group for the next week. You may see instructions for something to bring to your next group meeting.

How to Use the Digital Version of This Study Guide

If you view this study guide in its downloadable form on your tablet, phone, or even your desktop, you won't need to print it out unless you want to. Throughout the guide are areas where you can type directly into the guide. Also provided are convenient links that direct you to external resources, including Scripture passages and interactive activities.

Helpful Tip

For the best experience on Android™ platforms, please view this interactive study on Adobe Acrobat Reader DC®.

Introducing Scripture Hyperlinks

Scripture hyperlinks enhance your reading experience by providing a seamless way to explore and engage with the Word of God. As you scroll through the content, activating the hyperlinks to focal Scriptures will unlock a wealth of resources and features. These hyperlinks are available on *Biblia.com,* a comprehensive online platform for studying and accessing the Bible. Not only will you find various Bible translations listed, but you will also benefit from the clarity provided by red letters, indicating when Jesus Christ is being quoted.

1. By activating the hyperlink to a focal Scripture as you scroll down, you will also find other Bible translations listed.

2. *Biblia.com* also provides a graphic you can share on social media of the Scripture you are reading.

3. The Scriptures utilize red letters to indicate when Jesus Christ is being quoted, providing clarity in identifying the speaker.

4. At the end of the passage is a "read more" button. When activated, it displays the entire chapter, allowing you to read the highlighted Scripture within its context.

5. For those interested in delving deeper into the study of a highlighted Scripture, there is a "learn more" button. This option provides an in-depth exploration, explaining verse by verse the significance, context, and circumstances surrounding the words spoken. It may also include immersive elements such as videos to enhance your understanding.

A Tip for the Host

The study guide material is meant to be your servant, not your master. The point is not to race through the sessions but to take time to let God work in your lives. It is not necessary to "go around the circle" before you move on to the next question. Give people the freedom to speak, but don't insist on it or make it mandatory. Your group will enjoy deeper, more open sharing and discussion if people aren't pressured to speak up.

Week 1

INITIATE

FOLLOW JESUS' APPROACH

GAME PLAN

For Your Small Group Meeting

- Read the **INTRODUCTION** to Week 1 together as a group.

- Read the Luke 10:38–42 NIV and Matthew 13:1–9 NIV passages out loud.

- Answer the **DISCUSSION QUESTIONS** as a group.

- Engage with the **GROUP ACTIVITY** during your small group time.

- Close by following the **PRAYER DIRECTION** and the **ONE LAST THING**.

On Your Own Time

Listen to Episode 1 of the *Rediscovering the Lost Art of Friendship Podcast* featuring a conversation with Saddleback Church Teaching Pastor, Stacie Wood.

For Your Small Group Meeting

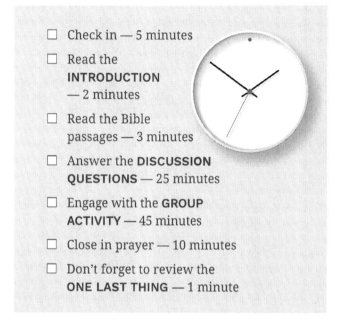

- ☐ Check in — 5 minutes
- ☐ Read the **INTRODUCTION** — 2 minutes
- ☐ Read the Bible passages — 3 minutes
- ☐ Answer the **DISCUSSION QUESTIONS** — 25 minutes
- ☐ Engage with the **GROUP ACTIVITY** — 45 minutes
- ☐ Close in prayer — 10 minutes
- ☐ Don't forget to review the **ONE LAST THING** — 1 minute

INITIATE

FOLLOW JESUS' APPROACH

⊞ INTRODUCTION

Welcome to Week 1 of *Rediscovering the Lost Art of Friendship*. Maybe you've noticed that meaningful and lasting friendships are declining around the world. And that decline is becoming more and more normal. From the dominance of social media to the polarization of ideas and opinions, it's clear that we're more distant from others relationally than ever before.

But now, maybe more than ever, we are becoming aware of our need for other people. God designed us for community. He created us for friendships.

As we begin this journey, it's essential that we start at the beginning, with the first step: initiating friendships. Maybe you can think of a time when you initiated a friendship. It might have been in grade school asking someone to play at recess, or perhaps you made friends with someone who shared a common interest later in life.

Somewhere along the way, it became harder to make new friends. But the good news is that God did not leave us without an example to follow.

Jesus was a master at initiating friendships. From calling the 12 disciples to sharing meals with strangers and outcasts, Jesus intentionally and consistently initiated friendships.

Sometimes it feels uncomfortable to initiate new conversations. We might feel timid or anxious. But as Jesus shows us, the risk is worth the reward when starting new friendships. This week's goal is to begin to imitate Jesus in how he lived his life and initiated friendships.

BIBLE READING

Have someone read both of the following passages out loud.

Luke 10:38–42 NIV

As Jesus and his disciples were on their way, he came to a village where a woman named Martha opened her home to him. ³⁹She had a sister called Mary, who sat at the Lord's feet listening to what he said. ⁴⁰But Martha was distracted by all the preparations that had to be made. She came to him and asked, "Lord, don't you care that my sister has left me to do the work by myself? Tell her to help me!"

⁴¹"Martha, Martha," the Lord answered, "you are worried and upset about many things, ⁴²but few things are needed—or indeed only one. Mary has chosen what is better, and it will not be taken away from her."

Matthew 13:1–9 NIV

That same day Jesus went out of the house and sat by the lake. ²Such large crowds gathered around him that he got into a boat and sat in it, while all the people stood on the shore. ³Then he told them many things in parables, saying: "A farmer went out to sow his seed. ⁴As he was scattering the seed, some fell along the path, and the birds came and ate it up. ⁵Some fell on rocky places, where it did not have much soil. It sprang up quickly, because the soil was shallow. ⁶But when the sun came up, the plants were scorched, and they withered because they had no root. ⁷Other seed fell among thorns, which grew up and choked the plants. ⁸Still other seed fell on good soil, where it produced a crop—a hundred, sixty or thirty times what was sown. ⁹Whoever has ears, let them hear."

The first passage is an example of how Mary and Martha initiated a friendship with Jesus. They opened their home, invited him in, and, in Mary's case, listened intently. The second passage is one typically used to illustrate evangelism. However, when you approach this passage through the lens of initiating friendship, some interesting principles emerge: 1) Not everyone you initiate friendship with will become a friend. Sometimes we resist creating friendship because we're afraid of rejection. Although that may happen, it shouldn't stop us from reaching out. 2) Not all friendships that start to grow will become deep, close bonds.

Some of those friendships will be bound to circumstances (like a class or a workplace) and when those circumstances change, the relationship will change, as well. Reach out anyway! 3) Some friendships will actually take root and grow and become life-giving and supportive.

🗨 DISCUSSION QUESTIONS

1. Jesus' closest friendships (outside of his 12 disciples) began with a simple invitation to a stranger. What do you imagine Martha thought or felt as she invited this group of 13 into her home? What would it look like for you to take the step to invite others into your home?

2. Mary chose what Jesus described as "better." What thoughts or feelings come up as you consider what this might mean for initiating friendships in your life?

3. What thoughts come to mind about the Parable of the Sower passage? Have you seen this principle play out in your life? If so, how?

👥 GROUP ACTIVITY

Strangers or Not?

OBJECTIVE: To create and foster connection with one another.

MATERIALS NEEDED: One die or access to an online dice roller. For digital readers go to *www.classtools.net/dice*

The game consists of three levels of questions aimed at helping each group member connect in an impactful manner. Each group member will answer one question per level.

Instructions

1. Beginning with Level 1 questions, each person takes turns to answer one question based on the die rolled.

2. The first person rolls the die and reads the correlating question to the group before answering the question.

3. The next person rolls the dice to see which question they will answer.

4. Continue until everyone has answered at least one question in Level 1.

5. Continue with Level 2 and then Level 3.

6. The game is complete when everyone has answered a question from each level.

Level 1: People

1. What was your childhood dream career?

2. If you had extra money, what would you splurge on?

3. What compliment do you hear the most?

4. What is your go-to karaoke song?

5. If you could have dinner with any person, who would it be?

6. What do your shoes tell us about you?

Level 2: Connection

1. What is something you wouldn't want to change about yourself?

2. What advice would you give to your younger self?

3. What is something you learned in the past year?

4. What title would you give this chapter in your life?

5. Whom are you surrounded by when you feel your best?

6. What's been your happiest memory this past year?

Level 3: Reflection

1. What kind of impact do you want to make in this lifetime?

2. What was the last thing you forgave yourself for?

3. What are you most grateful for in this current moment?

4. What do you admire in another member of the group?

5. What do you feel is your greatest strength to the group?

6. What goal do you have for yourself?

 ## PRAYER DIRECTION

As a group, thank God for bringing you together as a small group. Whether you have been together for many years or this is your first meeting, thank God for bringing you into each other's lives. Ask him to help you grow closer as friends and to see friendship in new, deeper ways. Thank God in advance for what he will do over the course of the next four sessions.

Each week, you are going to take turns praying over one or two people in your group. Choose one or two people, depending on how many in your group, knowing that this study is five weeks long. Then, take turns having the other people in your group pray for that individual. Thank God for that person, for how he made them unique, and ask God to bless their friendships and grow them as a friend to others.

🎙 REDISCOVERING THE LOST ART OF FRIENDSHIP PODCAST

On your own time, listen to Episode 1 of *Rediscovering the Lost Art of Friendship Podcast*, featuring a conversation with Saddleback  Church teaching pastor, Stacie Wood on what it looks like to make friends the way Jesus did. Use *sdbk.cc/friendship*, the QR code here, or search for *Rediscovering the Lost Art of Friendship* in your favorite podcast app.

✌ ONE LAST THING

Make sure to check out the **GAME PLAN** for Week 2, "Invest: Build a Strong Foundation," on page 27. For the Week 2 **GROUP ACTIVITY**, you will be sharing your story. It may be helpful to look at this in advance (page 48) to prepare for the activity.

Week 2

INVEST

BUILD A STRONG FOUNDATION

🎲 GAME PLAN

Before Your Small Group Meets

- Read the **INTRODUCTION** to Week 2.

- Listen to Episode 2 of the *Rediscovering the Lost Art of Friendship Podcast* featuring a conversation with Saddleback Church men's pastor, Anthony Miller.

- Follow the **DAILY BIBLE READING** plan for five days leading up to your small group meeting.

- Engage with the reflection questions for each Bible reading.

- Look ahead to this week's **GROUP ACTIVITY** (page 48). You will be sharing your story, and it may require some advance preparation.

During Your Small Group Meeting

- Answer the **DISCUSSION QUESTIONS** as a group.

- Engage with the **GROUP ACTIVITY** during your small group time.

- Close by following the **PRAYER DIRECTION** and the **ONE LAST THING**.

INVEST

BUILD A STRONG FOUNDATION

🗓 INTRODUCTION

If the first step to *Rediscovering the Lost Art of Friendship* is to initiate new conversations with people in your life, the second step is to begin investing in those friendships. Just like it doesn't make sense to open a new bank account and invest no money into it, friendships can only grow and develop if we invest in them.

Everything worthwhile takes intentionality and investment spent over time. That means building good friendships doesn't happen overnight. It is something that we do over time. Investing is indispensable to great friendships.

Over the next week, you and your group are going to learn some practical ways to invest in your friendships from God's Word. You'll learn from some great stories, like the account of Jesus and Lazarus, as well as a description of the early church. If you learn something new or have a great idea, put it into practice as soon as you can.

Don't wait for someone else to make the first move either. If you've initiated a friendship, take the next step to begin investing in that relationship. In what specific ways can you invest your time, resources, prayers, energy, or presence?

Remember, when we invest time in others, they also influence us. So take the time this week to learn how to invest wisely in friendships.

REDISCOVERING THE LOST ART OF FRIENDSHIP PODCAST

Listen to Episode 2 of the *Rediscovering the Lost Art of Friendship Podcast* featuring a conversation with Saddleback Church men's pastor, Anthony Miller, on what it looks like to build meaningful friendships through the investment of time, resources, and energy. Use *sdbk.cc/friendship*, the QR code here or search for *Rediscovering the Lost Art of Friendship* in your favorite podcast app.

DAILY BIBLE READING

Throughout this week, read and reflect on each of the five days of Bible reading. Then take time to consider and respond to each day's accompanying question(s).

Day 1

Acts 2:42–47 NLT

All the believers devoted themselves to the apostles' teaching, and to fellowship, and to sharing in meals (including the Lord's Supper), and to prayer.

[43]A deep sense of awe came over them all, and the apostles performed many miraculous signs and wonders. [44]And all the believers met together in one place and shared everything they had. [45]They sold their property and possessions and shared the money with those in need. [46]They worshiped together at the Temple each day, met in homes for the Lord's Supper, and shared their meals with great joy and generosity—[47]all the while praising God and enjoying the goodwill of all the people. And each day the Lord added to their fellowship those who were being saved.

Brought together by their new common faith, these believers began to invest in one another. They invested themselves, their time, their resources, and possessions into this new community. Today we'd say they were *"doing life together."* The love and care they shared was so powerful that it drew others in.

Reflect

Note the verbs used in the passage above. What does *"doing life together"* look like?

Being involved. Knowing.
Helping . Communicating
All actionable verbs.

Day 2

While Jesus had many disciples (followers), there were 12 specifically named apostles, with whom he invested significant time and training during his years of ministry.

Luke 8:1–3 NIV

After this, Jesus traveled about from one town and village to another, proclaiming the good news of the kingdom of God. The Twelve were with him, ²and also some women who had been cured of evil spirits and diseases: Mary (called Magdalene) from whom seven demons had come out; ³Joanna the wife of Chuza, the manager of Herod's household; Susanna; and many others. These women were helping to support them out of their own means.

Luke 9:1–2, 6 NIV

When Jesus had called the Twelve together, he gave them power and authority to drive out all demons and to cure diseases, ²and he sent them out to proclaim the kingdom of God and to heal the sick.

⁶So they set out and went from village to village, proclaiming the good news and healing people everywhere.

Matthew 20:17–19 NIV

Now Jesus was going up to Jerusalem. On the way, he took the Twelve aside and said to them, ¹⁸"We are going up to Jerusalem, and the Son of Man will be delivered over to the chief priests and the teachers of the law. They will condemn him to death ¹⁹and will hand him over to the Gentiles to be mocked and flogged and crucified. On the third day he will be raised to life!"

Luke 22:39–42 NIV

Jesus went out as usual to the Mount of Olives, and his disciples followed him. ⁴⁰On reaching the place, he said to them, "Pray that you will not fall into temptation." ⁴¹He withdrew about a stone's throw beyond them, knelt down and prayed, ⁴²"Father, if you are willing, take this cup from me; yet not my will, but yours be done."

It's easy to read through the gospels and assume that every time the word "disciple" is used that it's referring to the "twelve" that we're familiar with. However, upon closer reading, it becomes clear that Jesus had many disciples, both men and women. People in almost every town he visited chose to follow him. From among those, he chose twelve who would travel with him and receive extra training and instruction. These men were sent out on mission and given the power and authority to carry the ministry of Jesus all over

their world. These were the men to whom Jesus
first uttered the words of John 15:15 NIV:

*"I no longer call you servants, because a
servant does not know his master's business.
Instead, I have called you friends, for
everything that I learned from my Father
I have made known to you."*

The disciples are a great example of the difference
between acquaintances and friends. Jesus knew
and interacted with a lot of people. He had many
acquaintances. In fact, it's likely that many of
the people who considered themselves his
disciples were barely acquaintances. The Twelve
were different. The extra time and energy he
invested in the Twelve and the experiences they
shared together not only strengthened their
friendships but also gave them the perspective
and insight they'd need for what lay ahead.

Reflect

What do you observe about Jesus in these stories?

JESUS' ACTIONS	JESUS' WORDS

What do you suspect Jesus believes
about friendship?

What does your time and energy say about what
you believe about friendship?

Day 3

Jesus' friends, Mary, Martha, and Lazarus, lived in
Bethany, a small town two miles from Jerusalem.
Jesus ended up in Bethany frequently. He was
there before his triumphal entry (Mark 11:1), in
the days leading up to the cross (John 12), and just
before he ascended to heaven (Luke 24:50). Jesus
often retreated there after long days of ministry in
the city (i.e., Matthew 21:17). Over a period of three
years, these frequent visits served to deepen and
strengthen his friendship with Mary, Martha, and
Lazarus. The significance of these friendships is
revealed in two stories from the gospel of John—
the raising of Lazarus and Jesus' anointing
at Bethany.

John 11:1–3, 33–36 NLT

A man named Lazarus was sick. He lived in
Bethany with his sisters, Mary and Martha.
²This is the Mary who later poured the
expensive perfume on the Lord's feet and
wiped them with her hair. Her brother,
Lazarus, was sick. ³So the two sisters sent
a message to Jesus telling him, "Lord, your
dear friend is very sick."

³³When Jesus saw her weeping and saw the
other people wailing with her, a deep anger
welled up within him, and he was deeply
troubled. ³⁴"Where have you put him?"
he asked them.

They told him, "Lord, come and see." [35]Then Jesus wept. [36]The people who were standing nearby said, "See how much he loved him!"

John 12:1–3, 7 NLT

Six days before the Passover celebration began, Jesus arrived in Bethany, the home of Lazarus—the man he had raised from the dead. [2]A dinner was prepared in Jesus' honor. Martha served, and Lazarus was among those who ate with him. [3]Then Mary took a twelve-ounce jar of expensive perfume made from essence of nard, and she anointed Jesus' feet with it, wiping his feet with her hair. The house was filled with the fragrance.

When Judas protests,

[7]Jesus replied, "Leave her alone. She did this in preparation for my burial."

These two stories reveal a depth of intimacy between Jesus, Mary, Martha, and Lazarus that is unique to these friendships. When Lazarus was dying, the sisters sent word that his "dear friend" was sick. Other translations use phrases like "the one you love" or "the one for whom you have great affection." In the second story, as Jesus was preparing for what will undoubtedly be the most excruciating and painful days of his life, he was back at the home of Mary, Martha, and Lazarus—a place of safety and respite, a place he was known and understood. While his disciples struggled to comprehend what Jesus was telling them about his imminent betrayal and death sentence, it's evident that, amongst these three, there was clarity. Mary anointed Jesus with expensive perfume in preparation for his coming burial. These clearly weren't casual connections. Their friendships were built on the foundation of time spent together. It's clear that the more time you spend with someone, the stronger the foundation of that friendship will be.

Reflect

What qualities grow in a friendship as you spend time together? What diminishes?

Today, many people substitute time spent
connecting on digital platforms for time spent
physically together. What are the benefits of
digital connection, and what might be lost
or sacrificed?

Day 4

While Jesus spent much time with the twelve, he spent even more focused time with three disciples: Peter, James, and John.

Mark 5:35–42 NET

While he was still speaking, some people came from the leader's house saying, "Your daughter is dead. Why trouble the teacher any further?" 36But overhearing what they said, Jesus said to the leader of the synagogue, "Do not fear, only believe." 37He allowed no one to follow him except Peter, James, and John, the brother of James. 38When they came to the house of the leader of the synagogue, he saw a commotion, people weeping and wailing loudly. 39When he had entered, he said to them, "Why do you make a commotion and weep? The child is not dead but sleeping." 40And they laughed at him. Then he put them all outside, and took the child's father and mother and those who were with him, and went in where the child was. 41He took her by the hand and said to her, "Talitha cum," which means, "Little girl, get up!" 42And immediately the girl got up and began to walk about (she was twelve years of age). At this they were overcome with amazement.

Mark 9:2–8 NET

Six days later Jesus took with him Peter, James, and John and led them alone up a high mountain privately. And he was transfigured before them, ³and his clothes became radiantly white, more so than any launderer in the world could bleach them. ⁴Then Elijah appeared before them along with Moses, and they were talking with Jesus. ⁵So Peter said to Jesus, "Rabbi, it is good for us to be here. Let us make three shelters—one for you, one for Moses, and one for Elijah." ⁶(For they were afraid, and he did not know what to say.) ⁷Then a cloud overshadowed them, and a voice came from the cloud, "This is my one dear Son. Listen to him!" ⁸Suddenly when they looked around, they saw no one with them any more except Jesus.

Mark 14:32–34 NET

Then they went to a place called Gethsemane, and Jesus said to his disciples, "Sit here while I pray." ³³He took Peter, James, and John with him, and became very troubled and distressed. ³⁴He said to them, "My soul is deeply grieved, even to the point of death. Remain here and stay alert."

Jesus had very close relationships with Peter, James, and John. They were invited into sacred moments that no one else saw—moments of mystery and power and very personal, vulnerable moments that others might not have understood.

They also had some of the most intense interactions with Jesus—he called Peter "Satan" at one point (Matthew 16:23) and he nicknamed James and John the "Sons of Thunder" (Mark 3:17). He had to talk down their overzealous mom who was trying to secure seats next to Jesus in his kingdom (Matthew 20:21). John even referred to himself (in the third person) as "the disciple Jesus loved" (John 13:23). It was John to whom Jesus entrusted the care of his own mother upon his death (John 19:26). In Jesus' relationship with Peter, James, and John, we see that friendships invested in regularly and over a period of time develop a foundation of trust and care and become places where we are sharpened, encouraged, and comforted.

Reflect

What was the impact of Jesus' deliberate investment in Peter, James, and John?

Who are the "Peter, James, and John" in your life? What is one way you could further invest in those friendships?

Day 5

Hebrews 10:24–25 ESV

And let us consider how to stir up one another to love and good works, ²⁵not neglecting to meet together, as is the habit of some, but encouraging one another, and all the more as you see the Day drawing near.

Ecclesiastes 4:9–10 CEV

You are better having a friend than to be all alone, because then you will get more enjoyment out of what you earn. ¹⁰If you fall, your friend can help you up. But if you fall without having a friend nearby, you are really in trouble.

Romans 12:10, 13 VOICE

Live in true devotion to one another, loving each other as sisters and brothers. Be first to honor others by putting them first. . . . ¹³Share what you have with the saints, so they lack nothing; take every opportunity to open your life and home to others.

Together, these passages reinforce the themes we've seen in our reading this week—God's design for our relationships is that we invest ourselves— our time, our energy, and our resources—in those we call "friends." This is an active process that won't happen without intentionality and planning.

REDISCOVERING THE LOST ART OF FRIENDSHIP

Reflect

Think of one friend. What can you do to overcome any barriers (challenges, excuses we make, distance, etc.) that keep you from investing in this friendship?

BARRIERS/EXCUSES	IDEAS FOR OVERCOMING

For Your Small Group Meeting

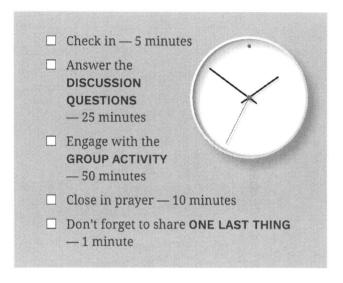

- ☐ Check in — 5 minutes
- ☐ Answer the **DISCUSSION QUESTIONS** — 25 minutes
- ☐ Engage with the **GROUP ACTIVITY** — 50 minutes
- ☐ Close in prayer — 10 minutes
- ☐ Don't forget to share **ONE LAST THING** — 1 minute

🗨 DISCUSSION QUESTIONS

1. Which passage from the Bible reading this week stood out to you the most and why?

2. Share a time when somebody invested in their relationship with you. What was it about their investment that makes it so memorable to you today?

3. What would you have to change to invest more time and energy into building friendships?

GROUP ACTIVITY

Three-Minute Testimony Sharing

As we get to know one another in our small groups, it is helpful to know each other's testimonies of how we came to know Jesus as our savior. Use the prompts below to craft your testimony. Then be prepared to share it with the group.

Instructions

1. Allow about 15 minutes for the group members to write out their testimonies.

2. Each person independently works on their testimony using the prompts below. Write or type it out.

3. When everyone is done or when time is up, go around the group and have each person share their testimony.

Three-Minute Testimony Prompts

1. Before I received Christ (1 minute):

   a. What was my life before I accepted Christ? If you received Christ at a very young age, you still have a story to tell! Focus on an area you struggled in after you were a believer.

   b. What did my life revolve around? What did I get my security or happiness from?

   c. How did those areas begin to let me down?

2. How I received Christ (1 minute):

   a. But then I realized I had an even bigger problem—my sin. When was the first time I heard the gospel? Or, when was I exposed to biblical Christianity?

   b. What were my initial reactions? When and how did I come to a decision?

3. After I received Christ (1 minute):

   a. Think of specific changes I have seen in my life (include personal illustrations of attitudes and actions since becoming a Christian). Share how understanding that your sin was/is completely paid for changed your perspective.

   b. How long did it take before I noticed changes?

   c. Why am I motivated differently? How does my relationship with Christ affect my decisions regarding activities, relationships, future, etc.?

Remember:

- Write as you speak—make the testimony yours!

- Choose a theme (i.e., insecurity, looking for success, loneliness, seeking meaning in life, looking for unconditional love, etc.).

- Don't ever feel like your story is boring. Every person's life relates to someone.

PRAYER DIRECTION

This week, take a few minutes to pray individually. Thank God for the people who have invested in building friendships with you. Mention them to God by name. Then, ask God to help you put a higher value on investing your time in building friendships. Ask him to point out areas in your life that can be done differently to free up more time for others.

When everyone is done praying individually, continue the prayer practice that started in week one. Choose another one or two people whom everyone will pray over. Then, take turns having the other people in your group pray for that individual. Thank God for that person, for how he made them unique, and ask God to bless their friendships and grow them as a friend to others.

 ## ONE LAST THING

Make sure to check out the **GAME PLAN** for Week 3, "Enrich: Experience God's Beautiful and Diverse Family," on page 53. The **GROUP ACTIVITY** for Week 3 requires advanced preparation. Consider reading the instructions (page 73) as a group now to prepare for next week.

Week 2: **INVEST**

Week 3

ENRICH

EXPERIENCE GOD'S BEAUTIFUL
AND DIVERSE FAMILY

GAME PLAN

Before Your Small Group Meets

- Read the **INTRODUCTION** to Week 3.

- Listen to Episode 3 of the *Rediscovering the Lost Art of Friendship Podcast* featuring a conversation with Transformation Church's lead pastor, Derwin Gray.

- Follow the **DAILY BIBLE READING** plan for five days leading up to your small group meeting.

- Engage with the reflection questions for each Bible reading.

- Look ahead to this week's **GROUP ACTIVITY** (page 73), as it requires some advance preparation.

During Your Small Group Meeting

- Answer the **DISCUSSION QUESTIONS** as a group.

- Engage with the **GROUP ACTIVITY** during your small group time.

- Close by following the **PRAYER DIRECTION** and the **ONE LAST THING**.

Week 3

ENRICH

EXPERIENCE GOD'S BEAUTIFUL AND DIVERSE FAMILY

INTRODUCTION

Maybe you've found one of the easiest ways to initiate new friends is by finding people who think the same way you do, act the same way you do and believe the same things you do. But what if that's not all that God intended for your friendships?

God designed people and communities diverse on purpose. When we're in community with people who look, think, and act differently than us, we're closer to God's design for our friendships. Even Jesus intentionally surrounded himself with a diverse group of friends.

When your friend group is made up of diverse backgrounds, ages, interests, experiences, and cultures, there's more wisdom and knowledge to share. There's more fun and excitement to enjoy. We actually grow and mature more when a diverse group of friends surrounds us than when we're all the same.

We're better when we're diverse!

Broadening our circle of friends takes intentionality and commitment, though. It requires us to stretch ourselves and widen our perspective. We must learn from others by listening. We'll need to adopt Jesus' mindset for how we consider others in our life.

Each day this week, take time to think about how you can be more like Jesus by enriching your friendships. Consider how you can build bridges of diversity in your friendships.

REDISCOVERING THE LOST ART OF FRIENDSHIP PODCAST

Listen to Episode 3 of the *Rediscovering the Lost Art of Friendship Podcast* featuring a conversation with Derwin Gray, lead pastor of Transformation  Church, on the biblical roots for diversity and the power of experiencing God's diverse family in your friendships. Use *sdbk.cc/friendship*, the QR code here, or search for *Rediscovering the Lost Art of Friendship* in your favorite podcast app.

DAILY BIBLE READING

Throughout this week, read and reflect on each of the five days of Bible reading. Then take time to consider and respond to each day's accompanying question(s).

Day 1

Luke 6:12–16 NIV

One of those days Jesus went out to a mountainside to pray, and spent the night praying to God. [13]*When morning came, he called his disciples to him and chose twelve of them, whom he also designated apostles:* [14]*Simon (whom he named Peter), his brother Andrew, James, John, Philip, Bartholomew,* [15]*Matthew* [a tax collector], *Thomas, James son of Alphaeus, Simon who was called the Zealot,* [16]*Judas son of James, and Judas Iscariot, who became a traitor.*

At first glance, this list of names isn't particularly striking, just twelve men Jesus selected as his designated apostles. However, the more you learn about them in the gospels, the more you realize just how dynamic and possibly explosive this group could have been. We know that Simon, Andrew, James, and John were fishermen— hard-working laborers and probably not highly educated. Judas Iscariot was good with money and became the treasurer of the group. Then we get to Simon, the Zealot. Zealots were a fiery group that hated Rome and its polytheism. And Matthew—a tax collector. Tax collectors were Jewish men who worked for the occupying Roman government. They collected the tax required from their countrymen and a little extra (sometimes a lot extra) for themselves. They were hated and seen

as traitors against their fellow Jews. Now the
picture looks a little different, doesn't it? Jesus
just named a bunch of guys to his team that, at
the outset, probably wouldn't have even chosen
to associate with one another. These men became
friends despite their differences when they first
came to Jesus. They traveled together, served
together, learned together, struggled together, and
eventually turned the world upside down for Jesus.

Reflect

Jesus disrupted the disciples' views of friendship.
If we're honest, we tend to surround ourselves
with people like us. What is unique or different
about Jesus' view of friendship?

What would need to change in your beliefs, thoughts, and feelings to be friends with someone very different from you?

Day 2

Ruth 1:1–5, 8–9, 16–18 NLT

In the days when the judges ruled in Israel, a severe famine came upon the land. So a man from Bethlehem in Judah left his home and went to live in the country of Moab, taking his wife and two sons with him. ²The man's name was Elimelech, and his wife was Naomi. Their two sons were Mahlon and Kilion. They were Ephrathites from Bethlehem in the land of Judah. And when they reached Moab, they settled there.

³Then Elimelech died, and Naomi was left with her two sons. ⁴The two sons married Moabite women. One married a woman named Orpah, and the other a woman named Ruth. But about ten years later, ⁵both Mahlon and Kilion died. This left Naomi alone, without her two sons or her husband.

⁸. . . Naomi said to her two daughters-in-law, "Go back to your mothers' homes. And may the LORD reward you for your kindness to your husbands and to me. ⁹May the LORD bless you with the security of another marriage." Then she kissed them good-bye, and they all broke down and wept.

¹⁶But Ruth replied, "Don't ask me to leave you and turn back. Wherever you go, I will go; wherever you live, I will live. Your people will be my people, and your God will be my God.

¹⁷Wherever you die, I will die, and there I will be buried. May the LORD punish me severely if I allow anything but death to separate us!" *¹⁸When Naomi saw that Ruth was determined to go with her, she said nothing more.*

Imagine what it would take to leave the only life you've ever known and move to a new country where the best you could be promised was subsistence living as one of the lowest members of society. That's exactly what Ruth does. Ruth was a Moabite woman. As God declared in Deuteronomy 23:3 NLT, the pagan Moabites could never enter the "assembly of the LORD"—the gathering of people who worshiped God at the Tabernacle or, later, at the Temple. Naomi was a Jewish widow. In ancient Israel, widowed women often had no inheritance (land or possessions) and were effectively destitute. The Mosaic Law provided for widows through the law of gleaning—picking through the fields to find what was left after the harvesters had completed their work. When Naomi suggested that her daughters-in-law return to their families, she did so, knowing that by returning, they would likely have the opportunity to marry again and have families of their own. Ruth's insistence on going with Naomi was powerful. She was leaving the possibility of a comfortable future in the home she knew to go to a place where she would be seen as "other." As a foreign widow, she would have had nothing, and because she was a Moabite, no self-respecting Jewish man would have ever wanted to marry her.

Ruth chose to stand with Naomi, to stay with her, and to walk toward an unknown future together. This reveals the depth of love and commitment they shared. Naomi must have certainly felt both humbled and deeply loved by Ruth. This kind of costly, sacrificial love enriched and strengthened their friendship.

Reflect

What potential risks might you face in broadening your friendships to include people who are very different from yourself?

While it may feel risky, what purposes can you imagine or see God has in asking us to enrich our friendships through diversity?

Day 3

Luke 19:1–10 NIV

*Jesus entered Jericho and was passing through.
²A man was there by the name of Zacchaeus;
he was a chief tax collector and was wealthy.
³He wanted to see who Jesus was, but because
he was short he could not see over the crowd.
⁴So he ran ahead and climbed a sycamore-fig
tree to see him, since Jesus was coming that way.*

*⁵When Jesus reached the spot, he looked up and
said to him, "Zacchaeus, come down immediately. I must stay at your house today." ⁶So he
came down at once and welcomed him gladly.*

*⁷All the people saw this and began to mutter,
"He has gone to be the guest of a sinner."*

*⁸But Zacchaeus stood up and said to the Lord,
"Look, Lord! Here and now I give half of my
possessions to the poor, and if I have cheated
anybody out of anything, I will pay back four
times the amount."*

*⁹Jesus said to him, "Today salvation has come
to this house, because this man, too, is a son of
Abraham. ¹⁰For the Son of Man came to seek
and to save the lost."*

When Jesus reached out to Zacchaeus, he did
more than acknowledge the man who had
climbed a tree to get a better view. Jesus reached
across social barriers and past expectations,

ignoring how it looked or what people might think. Zacchaeus was a hated tax collector for the Roman government. He regularly overcharged his fellow Jews to make himself rich. To associate with him at all, let alone share a meal, would have been seen as sacrilege, but Jesus reached out anyway. Jesus sets a powerful example of connecting with someone most would reject or avoid.

Reflect

Jesus reached out to Zacchaeus despite knowing what people might say or think about it. What do you think Jesus believes about friendship that allowed him to reach out anyway?

In what ways do you reflect Jesus' love by making friends with those different from you?

Day 4

John 4:3–26 NIV

So he left Judea and went back once more to Galilee.

⁴Now he had to go through Samaria. ⁵So he came to a town in Samaria called Sychar, near the plot of ground Jacob had given to his son Joseph. ⁶Jacob's well was there, and Jesus, tired as he was from the journey, sat down by the well. It was about noon.

⁷When a Samaritan woman came to draw water, Jesus said to her, "Will you give me a drink?" ⁸(His disciples had gone into the town to buy food.)

⁹The Samaritan woman said to him, "You are a Jew and I am a Samaritan woman. How can you ask me for a drink?" (For Jews do not associate with Samaritans.)

¹⁰Jesus answered her, "If you knew the gift of God and who it is that asks you for a drink, you would have asked him and he would have given you living water."

¹¹"Sir," the woman said, "you have nothing to draw with and the well is deep. Where can you get this living water? ¹² Are you greater than our father Jacob, who gave us the well and drank from it himself, as did also his sons and his livestock?"

¹³*Jesus answered, "Everyone who drinks this water will be thirsty again, ¹⁴but whoever drinks the water I give them will never thirst. Indeed, the water I give them will become in them a spring of water welling up to eternal life."*

¹⁵*The woman said to him, "Sir, give me this water so that I won't get thirsty and have to keep coming here to draw water."*

¹⁶*He told her, "Go, call your husband and come back."*

¹⁷*"I have no husband," she replied.*

Jesus said to her, "You are right when you say you have no husband. ¹⁸The fact is, you have had five husbands, and the man you now have is not your husband. What you have just said is quite true."

¹⁹*"Sir," the woman said, "I can see that you are a prophet. ²⁰Our ancestors worshiped on this mountain, but you Jews claim that the place where we must worship is in Jerusalem."*

²¹*"Woman," Jesus replied, "believe me, a time is coming when you will worship the Father neither on this mountain nor in Jerusalem. ²²You Samaritans worship what you do not know; we worship what we do know, for salvation is from the Jews. ²³Yet a time is coming and has now come when the true worshipers will worship the Father in the Spirit and in truth, for they are the kind of worshipers the*

Father seeks. [24]God is spirit, and his worshipers must worship in the Spirit and in truth."

[25]The woman said, "I know that Messiah" (called Christ) "is coming. When he comes, he will explain everything to us."

[26]Then Jesus declared, "I, the one speaking to you—I am he."

This entire conversation is shocking, and it's not because of what was said. There were two socio-cultural dynamics in play that make it an almost impossible scenario. The first has to do with the history between Jews and Samaritans. In verse 9 of this passage, John notes that "Jews do not associate with Samaritans." He's right. The Samaritan people were the result of intermarriage between rebellious Jews and pagan foreigners during the time of the Babylonian captivity. They were considered half-breeds and were hated by the Jews of Jesus' day. Jews and Samaritans intentionally avoided each other. The second dynamic is revealed by the fact that this woman is at the well "at about noon." Historically, the women drew water in the cool of the early morning and did it together. This woman was alone at the well in the middle of the day. Why? Because she was an outcast. She had five husbands and was currently living with a man to whom she was not married. This made the fact that Jesus didn't just speak to her but engaged her in full theological discussion all the more astounding. Through his behavior, he

REDISCOVERING THE LOST ART OF FRIENDSHIP

created an opportunity for friendship, all while
challenging significant and well-established social
and cultural norms.

Reflect

In our culture today, people are often being told
who they can and can't interact with. What would
it look like if we were able to see beyond labels
and initiate friendship the way Jesus did?

68

Day 5

Luke 10:25–37 ESV

And behold, a lawyer stood up to put him to the test, saying, "Teacher, what shall I do to inherit eternal life?" ²⁶He said to him, "What is written in the Law? How do you read it?" ²⁷And he answered, "You shall love the Lord your God with all your heart and with all your soul and with all your strength and with all your mind, and your neighbor as yourself." ²⁸And he said to him, "You have answered correctly; do this, and you will live."

²⁹But he, desiring to justify himself, said to Jesus, "And who is my neighbor?" ³⁰Jesus replied, "A man was going down from Jerusalem to Jericho, and he fell among robbers, who stripped him and beat him and departed, leaving him half dead. ³¹Now by chance a priest was going down that road, and when he saw him he passed by on the other side. ³²So likewise a Levite, when he came to the place and saw him, passed by on the other side. ³³But a Samaritan, as he journeyed, came to where he was, and when he saw him, he had compassion. ³⁴He went to him and bound up his wounds, pouring on oil and wine. Then he set him on his own animal and brought him to an inn and took care of him. ³⁵And the next day he took out two denarii and gave them to the innkeeper, saying, 'Take care of him, and whatever more

you spend, I will repay you when I come back.'
[36]Which of these three, do you think, proved
to be a neighbor to the man who fell among
the robbers?" [37]He said, "The one who
showed him mercy." And Jesus said to him,
"You go, and do likewise."

Jesus used the story of the Good Samaritan to teach
the religious Jewish leaders what it meant to love
their neighbor. Typically when this story is taught,
the Samaritan is highlighted as the exemplar of a
neighbor. However, two people in this story, the
Samaritan and the innkeeper, demonstrate what
it means to love their neighbor. The innkeeper is
only mentioned once and only in passing, but his
role is significant. The Samaritan has entrusted
the severely beaten man to the innkeeper's care.
It is now his responsibility to ensure that the man
receives the care he needs during his recovery
and recuperation. While it is true that his expenses
would be reimbursed by the Samaritan, the
innkeeper becomes a caretaker for a broken,
hurting man he doesn't know or have any
personal reason to care for or about.

Reflect

What would it look like for you to broaden to the broken—to make space for the hurting people Jesus brings to you?

For Your Small Group Meeting

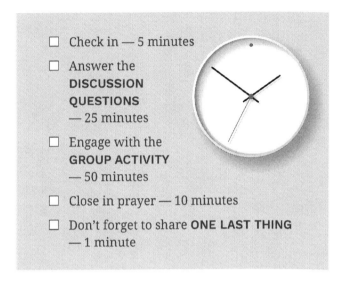

- ☐ Check in — 5 minutes
- ☐ Answer the **DISCUSSION QUESTIONS** — 25 minutes
- ☐ Engage with the **GROUP ACTIVITY** — 50 minutes
- ☐ Close in prayer — 10 minutes
- ☐ Don't forget to share **ONE LAST THING** — 1 minute

💬 DISCUSSION QUESTIONS

1. Which passage from the Bible reading this week stood out to you the most and why?

2. As you saw in the **DAILY BIBLE READING**, there are many ways to enrich your friend circle (generationally, racially, ethnically, politically, etc.). What is something that you have learned from a friend who is different from you that you would likely not have known otherwise?

3. Sometimes, people try to avoid talking about what makes them different from others. In what ways can we be more intentional about embracing our differences rather than avoiding them?

GROUP ACTIVITY

Show and Tell

NOTE: This activity requires advanced preparation.

Each one of us has a unique background and story of origin. Our lives are full of family stories or traditions. Use the group time to share about your family background or tradition.

Have each person share a "Show and Tell" option from the list below. Predetermine how much time each person needs to share in the group. (You will have about 50 minutes for this activity. If you have 10 members and each share for 5 minutes or if you have 5 members, each can share for 10 minutes.) Watch the time to make sure that everyone gets to share.

Show and Tell Options

1. Prepare a family recipe and share about the dish.
    a. Who created the recipe?
    b. When would the dish be served?
    c. What memories does the dish invoke?

2. Share your family history with a picture or two.
    a. Gather a few pictures of family members or memories.
    b. Share with the group who each person or memory is and what they mean to you.

3. Share a travel adventure.
   a. Gather a few photos or videos to show your travel adventures.
   b. Share how your travels have impacted you. What have you learned about the world or other cultures?

4. Share a family heirloom.
   a. Bring a family heirloom to the group or show the group online.
   b. Share the history of the heirloom and why it is important to you and your family.

After everyone has shared, reflect on the following questions:

1. What did you learn about one another?
2. What do you have in common with other group members?
3. Did this activity reflect the diversity of backgrounds within your group? If so, how?

PRAYER DIRECTION

As a group, thank God for making people so wonderfully diverse. Thank him for purposefully creating people to be so different from one another. Thank him for the differences in your very own group. Ask God to give you a better appreciation of the beautiful tapestry of humanity made of billions of different types of thread. Ask him to help you appreciate and value the differences in others and to not just bring different people into your life but to give you eyes to see them and a heart to reach out to them in friendship.

Then, continue the prayer practice that started in week one. Choose another one or two people whom everyone will pray over. Then, take turns having the other people in your group pray for that individual. Thank God for that person, for how he made them unique, and ask God to bless their friendships and grow them as a friend to others.

ONE LAST THING

Make sure to check out the **GAME PLAN** for Week 4, "Strengthen: Cultivate Openness and Honesty," on page 77.

Week 4

STRENGTHEN

CULTIVATE OPENNESS AND HONESTY

GAME PLAN

Before Your Small Group Meets

- Read the **INTRODUCTION** to Week 4.

- Listen to Episode 4 of the *Rediscovering the Lost Art of Friendship Podcast* featuring a conversation with Dr. Todd Hall, clinical psychologist and professor of psychology at Biola University.

- Follow the **DAILY BIBLE READING** plan for five days leading up to your small group meeting.

- Engage with the reflection questions for each Bible reading.

During Your Small Group Meeting

- Answer the **DISCUSSION QUESTIONS** as a group.

- Engage with the **GROUP ACTIVITY** during your small group time.

- Close by following the **PRAYER DIRECTION** and the **ONE LAST THING**.

STRENGTHEN

CULTIVATE OPENNESS
AND HONESTY

⊞ INTRODUCTION

Life is a journey. Maybe you can remember
the various experiences and trials you've had.
Some seasons are positive and full of great
memories; others are more difficult and require
more strength to endure.

What is certain, though, is that every season of life
is a good season to strengthen our friends because
we need strong friendships in every season of life.
Professional athletes don't wait for the first game
to begin strength training. They train all year
round so that they're ready for the next challenge
when it comes.

Similarly, we should always strengthen our
friendships so that when trouble and trials
come, we can prepare for the challenge together.
Maintaining our friendships can happen in a
variety of ways, like spending time together or
planning intentional activities. However, strength
often comes through vulnerability and hardship-
by being open and honest about what's happening

within us. Friendships built on a strong foundation can endure hardship together, support one another, and strengthen each other.

Jesus showed us how to be vulnerable in the Garden of Gethsemane. Additionally, from Job to Esther to the four friends who helped their friend get to Jesus for healing, God's Word can help us think through ways to strengthen our friendships.

How are you strengthening those around you? How are your friends supporting and building you up? If we're not intentionally strengthening our friends today, we won't be ready for what may come tomorrow.

REDISCOVERING THE LOST ART OF FRIENDSHIP PODCAST

Listen to Episode 4 of the *Rediscovering the Lost Art of Friendship Podcast* featuring a conversation with Dr. Todd Hall, clinical psychologist and professor of psychology at Biola University, on how openness and vulnerability in friendships lead to depth, trust, and tighter bonds. Use *sdbk.cc/friendship*, the QR code here, or search for *Rediscovering the Lost Art of Friendship* in your favorite podcast app.

DAILY BIBLE READING

Throughout this week, read and reflect on each of the five days of Bible reading. Then take time to consider and respond to each day's accompanying question(s).

Day 1

1 Samuel 18:1–4 NLT

After David had finished talking with Saul, he met Jonathan, the king's son. There was an immediate bond between them, for Jonathan loved David. ²From that day on Saul kept David with him and wouldn't let him return home. ³And Jonathan made a solemn pact with David, because he loved him as he loved himself. ⁴Jonathan sealed the pact by taking off his robe and giving it to David, together with his tunic, sword, bow, and belt.

1 Samuel 23:15–18 NLT

One day near Horesh, David received the news that Saul was on the way to Ziph to search for him and kill him. ¹⁶Jonathan went to find David and encouraged him to stay strong in his faith in God. ¹⁷"Don't be afraid," Jonathan reassured him. "My father will never find you! You are going to be the king of Israel, and I will be next to you, as my father, Saul, is well aware." ¹⁸So the two of them renewed their solemn pact before the Lord. Then Jonathan returned home, while David stayed at Horesh.

People are more likely to be open and vulnerable with those they know are committed to them. The first thing we learn about the friendship between David and Jonathan is that it was characterized by a deep commitment to one another. This covenant or pact has been defined by commentators as a covenant of friendship and peace that would last even beyond their lifetimes and extend to their descendants after them. The gifts that Jonathan gave David were extremely significant. The robe was likely Jonathan's kingly robe, symbolizing the handing over of succession to his father's throne. The gifts of the tunic, sword, bow, and belt were symbols of great honor.

The strength of their friendship is seen multiple times as King Saul makes several attempts on David's life. During these times, Jonathan repeatedly strengthened his commitment to friendship with David.

Reflect

How do you (or how could you) demonstrate commitment in your friendships?

Day 2

Over a span of just a few days, Job loses his children, his servants, his flocks, and his health. News of his suffering spread, and in Job 2:11–13 ESV we read:

Now when Job's three friends heard of all this evil that had come upon him, they came each from his own place, Eliphaz the Temanite, Bildad the Shuhite, and Zophar the Naamathite. They made an appointment together to come to show him sympathy and comfort him. ¹²And when they saw him from a distance, they did not recognize him. And they raised their voices and wept, and they tore their robes and sprinkled dust on their heads toward heaven. ¹³And they sat with him on the ground seven days and seven nights, and no one spoke a word to him, for they saw that his suffering was very great.

Few things draw our hearts closer together than entering into the pain of another. These verses paint a poignant picture of what it looks like to "show up and shut up." In the Jewish faith, there is a practice called "sitting shiva." Shiva means seven (referring to the prescribed seven days of mourning for the loss of a loved one), and to sit shiva literally describes mourners "sitting low" with a person as they process their grief. Job's friends did exactly that. They heard about his suffering, traveled to be with him, grieved with him, and then sat in silence with him for a week.

Verse 12 tells us that they wept loudly, tore their clothes, and sprinkled dust on their heads. In very real ways, they entered into his suffering. The comfort they offered came not through their words but through their presence.

Reflect

The Bible uses the phrase bearing or carrying another's burden (Galatians 6:2 ESV). In what ways have your friendships been strengthened through carrying or bearing burdens?

How can God use us when we are present to others in pain?

Day 3

Esther 4:6–16 CEV

Hathach went to Mordecai in the city square in front of the palace gate, [7]and Mordecai told him everything that had happened. He also told him how much money Haman had promised to add to the king's treasury if all the Jews were killed.

[8]Mordecai gave Hathach a copy of the orders for the murder of the Jews and told him that these had been read in Susa. He said, "Show this to Esther and explain what it means. Ask her to go to the king and beg him to have pity on her people, the Jews!"

[9]Hathach went back to Esther and told her what Mordecai had said. [10]She answered, "Tell Mordecai [11]there is a law about going in to see the king, and all his officials and his people know about this law. Anyone who goes in to see the king without being invited by him will be put to death. The only way that anyone can be saved is for the king to hold out the gold scepter to that person. And it's been thirty days since he has asked for me."

[12]When Mordecai was told what Esther had said, [13]he sent back this reply, "Don't think that you will escape being killed with the rest of the Jews, just because you live in the king's palace. [14]If you don't speak up now, we will somehow get help, but you and your family will be killed. It could be that you were made queen for a time like this!"

*¹⁵Esther sent a message to Mordecai, saying,
¹⁶"Bring together all the Jews in Susa and tell
them to go without eating for my sake! Don't eat
or drink for three days and nights. My servant
girls and I will do the same. Then I will go in to
see the king, even if it means I must die."*

Sometimes it's difficult to ask for help or admit
you're scared or feeling incapable of what is
ahead of you. In this story, Queen Esther has
a difficult choice to make. She must approach
the king, uninvited, to inform him of the plot
against her people, the Jews, which could result
in her death. OR she protects her own life, all but
ensuring the extinction of her people. She knows
that any hope of success will only come if God
helps her. She doesn't hide or mask her fear at all.
Instead, she enlists her servant girls (and all of the
Jews in Susa) to fast and pray for her so that she
can do what she needs to do.

Reflect

What changes in your thoughts and feelings when
you share your fears and insecurities with others
and ask them to pray with you and for you?

Day 4

Mark 2:1–5 ESV

And when he returned to Capernaum after some days, it was reported that he was at home. ²And many were gathered together, so that there was no more room, not even at the door. And he was preaching the word to them. ³And they came, bringing to him a paralytic carried by four men. ⁴And when they could not get near him because of the crowd, they removed the roof above him, and when they had made an opening, they let down the bed on which the paralytic lay. ⁵And when Jesus saw their faith, he said to the paralytic, "Son, your sins are forgiven."

Job 6:14 HCSB

A despairing man should receive loyalty from his friends, even if he abandons the fear of the Almighty.

When challenging circumstances persist, it's easy for our faith to wane. The paralytic man had probably been paralyzed for many years, maybe his whole life. It's hard to say, but what we know for sure is that he obviously couldn't come to Jesus on his own. His four friends loaded him up on a mat and then literally destroyed the roof of someone's house to get him to Jesus. Mark tells us that Jesus observed and honored the faith of his friends, and because of that, he healed the man.

They believed and came to Jesus on his behalf when he couldn't or didn't. They physically interceded for him to bring him to the one who was able to help when nothing and no one else could. Sometimes we become paralyzed by fear, or anger, or indecision, and we can't (or just don't) come to Jesus on our own. In those moments, we need friends who will step in to carry us—to have faith in us.

Reflect

In what ways might it strengthen your friendships to allow yourself to be "carried" by others?

Day 5

Mark 14:32–42 CEV

Jesus went with his disciples to a place called Gethsemane, and he told them, "Sit here while I pray."

33Jesus took along Peter, James, and John. He was sad and troubled and 34told them, "I am so sad that I feel as if I am dying. Stay here and keep awake with me."

35-36Jesus walked on a little way. Then he knelt down on the ground and prayed, "Father, if it is possible, don't let this happen to me! Father, you can do anything. Don't make me suffer by drinking from this cup. But do what you want, and not what I want."

37When Jesus came back and found the disciples sleeping, he said to Simon Peter, "Are you asleep? Can't you stay awake for just one hour? 38Stay awake and pray that you won't be tested. You want to do what is right, but you are weak."

39Jesus went back and prayed the same prayer. 40But when he returned to the disciples, he found them sleeping again. They simply could not keep their eyes open, and they did not know what to say.

41When Jesus returned to the disciples the third time, he said, "Are you still sleeping and resting? Enough of this! The time has come for the Son of Man to be handed over to sinners.

⁴²Get up! Let's go. The one who will betray me is already here."

In Luke's parallel account, we get a detail that helps us imagine the depths of Jesus' anguish. This occurs right before Jesus returns to find the disciples sleeping for the final time.

Luke 22:44 NIV

And being in anguish, he prayed more earnestly, and his sweat was like drops of blood falling to the ground.

This was the darkest moment of Jesus' life up to this point. He knew what was ahead of him, and, in his humanity, he cried out to God three different times, begging for the "cup to pass from him." In other words, Jesus was saying, "If there's any other way for this to go down, now would be a great time to let me know what that is." The Father was silent. This was the way it had to be. So great was Jesus' stress and anguish that Luke tells us his sweat was tinged with blood. It's significant that Jesus didn't go to the Garden of Gethsemane alone. He didn't try to hide what he was feeling. His disciples were with him. Sometimes, when faced with something deeply painful or challenging, for lots of reasons, we opt to isolate instead of reaching out. But Jesus shows us that in moments like this, we need our friends more than ever.

Reflect

In what ways might you become more open and honest in your friendships? What benefit might come as a result?

For Your Small Group Meeting

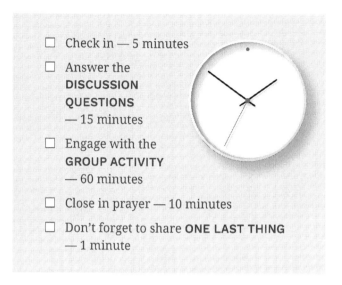

- ☐ Check in — 5 minutes
- ☐ Answer the **DISCUSSION QUESTIONS** — 15 minutes
- ☐ Engage with the **GROUP ACTIVITY** — 60 minutes
- ☐ Close in prayer — 10 minutes
- ☐ Don't forget to share **ONE LAST THING** — 1 minute

🗨 DISCUSSION QUESTIONS

1. Which passage from the Bible reading this week stood out to you the most and why?

2. How have you generally approached openness and vulnerability? Would people say you're an open book, guarded, or somewhere in between? Why do you think that is?

3. How would you define the type of person you would trust being open and vulnerable with? How could you grow to be more of that type of person for somebody else?

GROUP ACTIVITY

Peaks and Valleys

The person you are now is partly a result of everything that has happened to you in the past: who you were with, where you have been, what you have done, and the outside events that have affected your life. We learn from the peaks and valleys of life—the good and bad experiences.

Small groups should be places where we can be open and vulnerable about who we are and what we have experienced in life. Vulnerability takes time to build within a group and requires us to take a bit of risk when sharing within our group.

Build vulnerability by sharing both peak and valley life experiences. For some, we are not ready to share our deepest pains, and that is okay. Share what is comfortable for you.

Instructions

1. Spend 5 to 10 minutes individually listing 3 to 5 peak (positive) experiences and 3 to 5 valley (negative) experiences. Jot them down in your phone or on some scratch paper.

2. Go around the group and share the experiences with one another.

3. After each person shares their experiences, have one person affirm them.

PRAYER DIRECTION

As a group, pray for a culture of openness, vulnerability, and care to exist in your small group. Ask God to help make your group a safe place and to give each of you the peace and courage to step out in sharing in deeper ways. Ask God to continue to grow each of you into the type of person that cares and can be trusted. Thank him for being at work in your group—helping to strengthen and deepen your bonds of friendship.

Then, continue the prayer practice that started in week one. Choose another one or two people whom everyone will pray over. Then, take turns having the other people in your group pray for that individual. Thank God for that person, for how he made them unique, and ask God to bless their friendships and grow them as a friend to others.

 ## ONE LAST THING

Make sure to check out the **GAME PLAN** for Week 5, "Discern: Select the Right Friends," on page 97. The **GROUP ACTIVITY** for Week 5 is to have a Gratitude Dinner during your small group meeting. Consider reading the instructions now (page 118) for next week's **GROUP ACTIVITY**.

Week 5

DISCERN

SELECT THE RIGHT FRIENDS

🎲 GAME PLAN

Before Your Small Group Meets

- Read the **INTRODUCTION** to Week 5.

- Listen to Episode 5 of the *Rediscovering the Lost Art of Friendship Podcast* featuring a conversation with Celebrate Recovery® pastor, Meaghan Grider.

- Follow the **DAILY BIBLE READING** plan for five days leading up to your small group meeting.

- Engage with the reflection questions for each Bible reading.

- Look ahead to this week's **GROUP ACTIVITY** (page 118), as a Gratitude Dinner requires advance preparation.

During Your Small Group Meeting

- Answer the **DISCUSSION QUESTIONS** as a group.

- Engage with the **GROUP ACTIVITY** during your small group time.

- Close by following the **PRAYER DIRECTION**.

DISCERN

SELECT THE RIGHT FRIENDS

⊞ INTRODUCTION

You've made it to Week 5 of *Rediscovering the Lost Art of Friendship*. Our hope is that the past few weeks have helped you form new friends, broaden your perspectives, and strengthen existing friendships.

This week might be the most important.

We all need discernment in the friends we surround ourselves with. Maybe you've found yourself in a place you never expected because of the people you spend time with. Our friends are a choice God gives us, so we need to think carefully about where we invest our time.

Influence goes both ways. We are all shaped and influenced by the friends we surround ourselves with, and we also shape and influence those around us. This is how God designed it so that we all become the type of people God wants us to be.

There is great danger, however, in friends who influence us in the wrong direction. Just like a rotten apple can ruin a whole bunch of apples, a bad friend can have devastating consequences. When people with bad character surround us, we can find ourselves gossiping, cheating, and dishonoring God by how we live.

On the other hand, when we have friends who encourage us, strengthen us, and sharpen our character, we begin to act more and more like Jesus. Scripture tells us God will give wisdom to those who ask—and all of us need wise judgment when it comes to our friends.

Discernment is essential in building lasting friendships, so take some time this week to reflect on God's Word to hone your skills at discernment.

REDISCOVERING THE LOST ART OF FRIENDSHIP PODCAST

Listen to Episode 5 of the *Rediscovering the Lost Art of Friendship Podcast* featuring a conversation with Celebrate Recovery pastor, Meaghan Grider on  the difficult yet important practice of discernment in friendships. Use *sdbk.cc/friendship*, the QR code here, or search for *Rediscovering the Lost Art of Friendship* in your favorite podcast app.

DAILY BIBLE READING

Throughout this week, read and reflect on each of the five days of Bible reading. Then take time to consider and respond to each day's accompanying question(s).

Day 1

Psalm 1:1–3 NLT

Oh, the joys of those who do not follow the advice of the wicked, or stand around with sinners, or join in with mockers. ²But they delight in the law of the LORD, meditating on it day and night.

³They are like trees planted along the riverbank, bearing fruit each season. Their leaves never wither, and they prosper in all they do.

Psalm 101:5–8 CEV

Anyone who spreads gossip will be silenced, no one who is conceited will be my friend.

⁶I will find trustworthy people to serve as my advisors; only an honest person will serve as an official. ⁷No one who cheats or lies will have a position in my royal court. ⁸Each morning I will silence any lawbreakers I find in the countryside or in the city of the LORD.

Psalm 26:4–5 GW

I did not sit with liars, and I will not be found among hypocrites. ⁵I have hated the mob of evildoers and will not sit with wicked people.

As you begin to think about curating friends and influences, it's important to remember that this isn't about separating yourself entirely from every negative or non-God-honoring person in your world. That would make carrying out the Great Commission (Matthew 28:16–20) virtually impossible. What we're talking about here is understanding the powerful influence that the people we spend time with wields in our lives and then making wise choices about who we spend the most time with. Like it or not, we become like the people we surround ourselves with. For better or worse, we are shaped by the people we spend our time with. 1 Corinthians 15:33 HCSB says, *"Bad company corrupts good morals."* We'd all like to believe this isn't true—that we are strong or mature enough to avoid being influenced or tempted by the behavior of others, but that's just not the case most of the time. This is why Solomon reminds us in Proverbs 12:26 NIV that, *"The righteous choose their friends carefully."*

Reflect

What do these Psalms say about who we choose as our friends?

Day 2

2 Chronicles 10:1–19 NET

Rehoboam traveled to Shechem, for all Israel had gathered in Shechem to make Rehoboam king. ²When Jeroboam son of Nebat heard the news, he was still in Egypt, where he had fled from King Solomon. Jeroboam returned from Egypt. ³They sent for him, and Jeroboam and all Israel came and spoke to Rehoboam, saying, ⁴"Your father made us work too hard! Now if you lighten the demands he made and don't make us work as hard, we will serve you." ⁵He said to them, "Go away for three days, then return to me." So the people went away.

⁶King Rehoboam consulted with the older advisers who had served his father Solomon when he had been alive. He asked them, "How do you advise me to answer these people?" ⁷They said to him, "If you are fair to these people, grant their request, and are cordial to them, they will be your servants from this time forward." ⁸But Rehoboam rejected their advice and consulted the young advisers who served him, with whom he had grown up. ⁹He asked them, "How do you advise me to respond to these people who said to me, 'Lessen the demands your father placed on us'?" ¹⁰The young advisers with whom Rehoboam had grown up said to him, "Say this to these people who have said to you, 'Your father made us

*work hard, but now lighten our burden'—
say this to them: 'I am a lot harsher than my
father!* [11]*My father imposed heavy demands on
you; I will make them even heavier. My father
punished you with ordinary whips; I will punish
you with whips that really sting your flesh.'"*

[12]*Jeroboam and all the people reported to
Rehoboam on the third day, just as the king
had ordered when he said, "Return to me on
the third day."* [13]*The king responded to the
people harshly. He rejected the advice of the
older men* [14]*and followed the advice of the
younger ones. He said, "My father imposed
heavy demands on you; I will make them even
heavier. My father punished you with ordinary
whips; I will punish you with whips that really
sting your flesh."* [15]*The king refused to listen to
the people, because God was instigating this
turn of events so that he might bring to pass
the prophetic announcement he had made
through Ahijah the Shilonite to Jeroboam
son of Nebat.*

[16]*When all Israel saw that the king refused to
listen to them, the people answered the king,
"We have no portion in David—no share in the
son of Jesse! Return to your homes, O Israel!
Now, look after your own dynasty, O David!" So
all Israel returned to their homes.* [17]*(Rehoboam
continued to rule over the Israelites who lived
in the cities of Judah.)* [18]*King Rehoboam sent
Hadoram, the supervisor of the work crews,
out after them, but the Israelites stoned him*

to death. King Rehoboam managed to jump into his chariot and escape to Jerusalem. ¹⁹So Israel has been in rebellion against the Davidic dynasty to this very day.

King Rehoboam rejected the good counsel of his kingly advisors and instead, consulted with his buddies. They appealed to his desire for power and control and counseled him to make things even harder for the people of Israel, which he did. It caused a great split in the nation of Israel that existed until both Israel and Judah went into captivity. King Rehoboam's dad, King Solomon, knew something that apparently Rehoboam didn't. In Proverbs 13:20 NLT, Solomon wrote, *"Walk with the wise and become wise; associate with fools and get in trouble."*

Reflect

How do you choose (discern) wise people to walk with?

What character traits or behavior patterns do you look for to discern if someone will be a good/ positive influence in your life?

Day 3

When we met Job's friends a couple of weeks ago, we saw the way they came alongside him and sat shiva with him as he grieved unimaginable losses. In that, they set an example for us to follow. However, as soon as they opened their mouths, things went downhill fast! Each brought scathing assessments of Job and tried to explain why he was suffering.

ELIPHAZ'S ACCUSATION

Job 4:5-8 NLT

But now when trouble strikes, you lose heart.
You are terrified when it touches you.

⁶Doesn't your reverence for God give
you confidence?
Doesn't your life of integrity give you hope?

⁷"Stop and think! Do the innocent die?
When have the upright been destroyed?

⁸My experience shows that those who plant
trouble and cultivate evil will harvest the same.

It's as if Eliphaz is saying, "God doesn't punish good people. If you're experiencing this kind of trouble, it must be because of something you did."

BILDAD'S ACCUSATION

Job 8:2–6 NLT

"How long will you go on like this?
You sound like a blustering wind.

³Does God twist justice?
Does the Almighty twist what is right?

⁴Your children must have sinned against him,
so their punishment was well deserved.

⁵But if you pray to God
and seek the favor of the Almighty,

⁶and if you are pure and live with integrity,
he will surely rise up and restore your
happy home.

It's as if Bildad is saying, "Clearly, you and your kids sinned. Whatever you did, if you just repent, God will make everything better."

ZOPHAR'S ACCUSATION

Job 11:6b, 13–17 NLT

Listen! God is doubtless punishing you
far less than you deserve!

¹³If only you would prepare your heart
and lift up your hands to him in prayer!

¹⁴Get rid of your sins,
and leave all iniquity behind you.

¹⁵Then your face will brighten with innocence.
You will be strong and free of fear.

¹⁶You will forget your misery;
it will be like water flowing away.

¹⁷Your life will be brighter than the noonday.
Even darkness will be as bright as morning.

It's as if Zophar is saying, "You deserve even worse than this! If you'd just pray and worship more, you'd forget your pain, and everything will be great again."

As readers of the book of Job, we have a perspective that neither Job nor his friends had. We know that what Job experienced was something God allowed after Satan accused him in God's presence of only worshiping God because he had blessed him. The more Job's friends attempted to explain his suffering, the worse he felt. Remember, Job's friends intended to comfort him. They probably had no idea how cruel their words sounded in his ears. Finally, in Job 16:2 NLT, he cries out, *"I have heard all this before. What miserable comforters you are!"*

Reflect

In what ways might you demonstrate wise discernment in how and when you choose to speak into a friend's life?

Day 4

Friendship is a two-way street—we are influenced and shaped by our friends, and they are influenced and shaped by us. In order to curate our friends wisely, we must not only be aware of the influence of others but also of the influence we have in others' lives. Not only do we become like those we spend time with, but we also tend to attract people like us. Let today's verses become both a filter for the kinds of people you're spending time with and a mirror for the person you are in your friendships.

Proverbs 17:9 NRSV

One who forgives an affront fosters friendship, but one who dwells on disputes will alienate a friend.

Proverbs 22:24–25 NIV

Do not make friends with a hot-tempered person, do not associate with one easily angered,

25or you may learn their ways and get yourself ensnared.

Proverbs 16:28 NIV

A perverse person stirs up conflict, and a gossip separates close friends.

Romans 12:10 ESV

Love one another with brotherly affection.
Outdo one another in showing honor.

Proverbs 27:9 ESV

Oil and perfume make the heart
glad, and the sweetness of a friend
comes from his earnest counsel.

Colossians 3:13 NIV

Bear with each other and forgive one another
if any of you has a grievance against someone.
Forgive as the Lord forgave you.

Job 16:20–21 NIV

My intercessor is my friend as my eyes pour
out tears to God; [21]on behalf of a man he
pleads with God as one pleads for a friend.

Reflect

Think about the most significant friendships in your life today.

How are your friends' behavioral patterns shaping you?

How are your behavioral patterns shaping your friends?

Day 5

Proverbs 13:20 NIV

Walk with the wise and become wise, for a companion of fools suffers harm.

Galatians 5:22–23 ESV

But the fruit of the Spirit is love, joy, peace, patience, kindness, goodness, faithfulness, [23]gentleness, self-control.

Proverbs 13:20 NIV reminds us of the power of those we surround ourselves with. We will become like those we spend time with. The question then is, how do we decide? What character traits or qualities do we look for in a person to determine if building a friendship with them is a wise decision? A great place to start is by looking at the fruit of their life. In other words, what is the character of their life? What do you observe about the way this person treats other people, how they approach their life, and how they deal with difficulties? In Galatians 5:22–23 ESV, Paul lists nine qualities that will characterize the life of someone walking by the Spirit. This person will exemplify these qualities in increasing measure. These are the kind of friends we want to have.

On this final day in *Rediscovering the Lost Art of Friendship*, take time to pray and reflect on all you've learned over the last five weeks. As you reflect on all five weeks of this study, what are your top takeaways about friendship?

Now, complete the chart below:

I'M CALLED TO . . .	WHAT WILL I DO?
initiate new friendships	
invest in my friendships	
enrich my circle of friendships	
strengthen my friendships	
discern in my friendships	

Finish this day by praying this prayer.

Heavenly Father,

Thank you for creating friendship. Help me to be the kind of friend you've called me to be. Give me the courage to initiate new friendships. Help me prioritize time with the people you've put in my life so those friendships can grow. Open my eyes so I can see those who are different from me, the way you see them, and can find bridges to build friendships with them. Show me how to move past fear to be open and authentic in my friendships, and may I be the kind of person who holds what others share with compassion. Finally, I pray for the wisdom to surround myself with people who will help me grow in my relationship with You.

In Jesus' name,
Amen

For Your Small Group Meeting

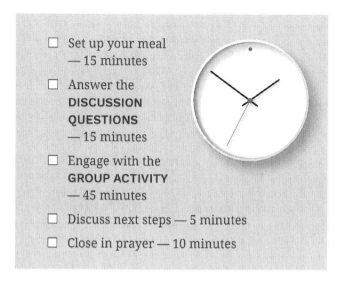

- ☐ Set up your meal — 15 minutes
- ☐ Answer the **DISCUSSION QUESTIONS** — 15 minutes
- ☐ Engage with the **GROUP ACTIVITY** — 45 minutes
- ☐ Discuss next steps — 5 minutes
- ☐ Close in prayer — 10 minutes

📖 DISCUSSION QUESTIONS

1. Which passage from the Bible reading this week stood out to you the most and why?

2. Take all five weeks of this study into consideration. How would you define the type of friend you should be, and what should your friendships look like?

3. How might deepening your friendship with Jesus help you grow your friendship with others?

GROUP ACTIVITY

Celebrate Your Friendships

Use the final week of this study to celebrate the friendships that have been established or deepened over the last several weeks. Host a Gratitude Dinner to uplift one another, cherish the connections, and express heartfelt gratitude for one another. The Gratitude Dinner could be a potluck, a picnic, a meal at a restaurant, or cooking a meal together. Be creative!

During or after the meal, spend some time expressing gratitude to one another using the following prompts:

- Express gratitude for a quality or trait that you admire in another person and how it has positively impacted your life.

- Reflect on a time when someone in the group provided support or encouragement that you are grateful for.

- Share a moment when someone in the group made you feel appreciated or loved, and express your gratitude for it.

- Express gratitude for a personal growth or positive change you have witnessed in one of the group members.

PRAYER DIRECTION

As a group, take some time to thank God for the gift of friendships. Thank him for making us to be personal, relational beings. Thank him for your small group—for the people he brought together for such a time as this study. Ask God to continue helping you grow in your friendships as a group and your friendships outside of your group. Pray that he will continue growing you as a friend to others.

Then, finish the prayer practice that started in week one. Choose the final person or people whom everyone will pray over. Then, take turns having the other people in your group pray for that individual. Thank God for that person, for how he made them unique, and ask God to bless their friendships and grow them as a friend to others.

Small Group Resources

Helps for Hosts *122*

Frequently Asked Questions *128*

Small Group Guidelines *130*

Circles of Life *132*

Prayer and Praise Report *133*

Small Group Calendar *134*

Additional Resources *135*

Small Group Roster *139*

Helps for Hosts

CONGRATULATIONS! As the host of your small group, you have responded to the call to help shepherd Jesus' flock. Few other tasks in the family of God surpass the contribution you will be making. As you prepare to facilitate your group, whether it is one session or the entire series, here are a few thoughts to keep in mind. Remember, you are not alone. God knows everything about you and knew you would be asked to facilitate your group. You may not feel ready; this is common for all good hosts. God promises, *"I will never leave you; I will never abandon you"* (Hebrews 13:5 NCV). Whether you are facilitating for one evening, several weeks, or a lifetime, you will be blessed as you serve.

Top Ten Ideas for New Hosts

1. **DON'T TRY TO DO IT ALONE.** Pray right now for God to help you build a healthy team. If you can enlist a cohost to help you shepherd the group, you will find your experience much richer. This is your chance to involve as many people as you can in building a healthy group. All you have to do is ask people to help. You'll be surprised at the response.

2. **BE FRIENDLY AND BE YOURSELF.** God wants to use your unique gifts and temperament. Be sure to greet people at the door with a big smile. This can set the mood for the whole gathering. Remember, they are taking as big of a step to show up for this study as you are to host a small group! Don't try to do things exactly like another host; do them in

a way that fits you. Admit when you don't have an answer, and apologize when you make a mistake. Your group will love you for it, and you'll sleep better at night.

3. **PREPARE FOR YOUR MEETING AHEAD OF TIME.** Review the session and write down your responses to each question. Pay special attention to the **GROUP ACTIVITY** each week. These activities are the bedrock for growing deeper friendships within your small group during this study.

4. **PRAY FOR YOUR GROUP MEMBERS BY NAME.** Before your group arrives, take a few moments and pray for each member by name. You may want to review the **PRAYER AND PRAISE REPORT** on page 133 at least once a week. Ask God to use your time together to touch the heart of each person in your group. Expect God to lead you to whomever he wants you to encourage or challenge in a special way. If you listen, God will surely lead.

5. **WHEN YOU ASK A QUESTION, BE PATIENT.** Someone will eventually respond. Sometimes people need a moment or two of silence to think about the question. If silence doesn't bother you, it won't bother anyone else. After someone responds, affirm the response with a simple "Thanks" or "Great answer." Then ask, "How about somebody else?" or "Would someone who hasn't shared like to add anything?" Be sensitive to new people or reluctant members who aren't ready to say, pray, or do anything. If you give them a safe setting, they will blossom over time. If someone in your group

is a wallflower who sits silently through every session, consider talking to that person privately and encouraging them to participate. Let them know how important they are to you—that they are loved and appreciated and that the group would value their input. Remember, still water often runs deep.

6. **PROVIDE TRANSITIONS BETWEEN QUESTIONS.** Ask if anyone would like to read a paragraph or Bible passage. Don't call on anyone, but ask for a volunteer, and then be patient until someone begins. Be sure to thank the person who reads aloud.

7. **BREAK INTO SMALLER GROUPS OCCASIONALLY.** With a greater opportunity to talk in a small circle, people will connect more with the study, apply more quickly what they're learning, and ultimately get more out of their small group experience. A small circle also encourages a quiet person to participate and tends to minimize the effects of a more vocal or dominant member.

8. **SMALL CIRCLES ARE ALSO HELPFUL DURING PRAYER TIME.** People unaccustomed to praying aloud will feel more comfortable trying it with just two or three others. Also, prayer requests won't take as much time, so circles will have more time to actually pray. When you gather back with the whole group, you can have one person from each circle briefly update everyone on the prayer requests from their subgroups. The other great aspect of subgrouping is that it fosters leadership

development. As you ask people in the group to facilitate discussion or to lead a prayer circle, it gives them a small leadership step that can build their confidence.

9. **ROTATE FACILITATORS OCCASIONALLY.** You may be perfectly capable of hosting each time, but you will help others grow in their faith and gifts if you give them opportunities to host the group.

10. **ONE FINAL CHALLENGE (FOR NEW OR FIRST-TIME HOSTS).** Before your first opportunity to lead, look up each of the six passages below. Read each as a devotional exercise to help prepare you with a shepherd's heart. Trust us on this one. If you do this, you will be more than ready for your first meeting.

Matthew 9:36–38 NIV

When [Jesus] *saw the crowds, he had compassion on them, because they were harassed and helpless, like sheep without a shepherd. [37]Then he said to his disciples, "The harvest is plentiful but the workers are few. [38]Ask the Lord of the harvest, therefore, to send out workers into his harvest field."*

John 10:14–15 NIV

"I am the good shepherd; I know my sheep and my sheep know me—[15]just as the Father knows me and I know the Father—and I lay down my life for the sheep."

1 Peter 5:2–4 NIV

Be shepherds of God's flock that is under your care, serving as overseers—not because you must, but because you are willing, as God wants you to be; not greedy for money, but eager to serve; ³not lording it over those entrusted to you, but being examples to the flock. ⁴And when the Chief Shepherd appears, you will receive the crown of glory that will never fade away.

Philippians 2:1–5 NIV

Therefore if you have any encouragement from being united with Christ, if any comfort from his love, if any common sharing in the Spirit, if any tenderness and compassion, ²then make my joy complete by being like-minded, having the same love, being one in spirit and of one mind. ³Do nothing out of selfish ambition or vain conceit. Rather, in humility value others above yourselves, ⁴not looking to your own interests but each of you to the interests of others. ⁵In your relationships with one another, have the same mindset as Christ Jesus.

Hebrews 10:23–25 NIV

Let us hold unswervingly to the hope we profess, for he who promised is faithful. ²⁴And let us consider how we may spur one another on toward love and good deeds, ²⁵not giving up meeting together as some are in the habit of doing, but encouraging one another—and all the more as you see the Day approaching.

1 Thessalonians 2:7–8, 11–12 NCV

We were very gentle with you, like a mother caring for her little children. ⁸Because we loved you, we were happy to share not only God's Good News with you, but even our own lives. You had become so dear to us!

¹¹You know that we treated each of you as a father treats his own children. ¹²We encouraged you, we urged you, and we insisted that you live good lives for God, who calls you to his glorious kingdom.

Frequently Asked Questions

How Long Will This Group Meet?

This study is five sessions long. In your final session, each group member may decide to continue to another study. At that time, you may also want to do some informal evaluation, discuss your group guidelines, and decide which study you want to do next. We recommend you visit our website at *saddleback.com/ studies* for more small group studies or search for the title on Amazon.

Who Is the Host?

The host is the person who coordinates and facilitates your group meetings. In addition to a host, we encourage you to select one or more group members to lead your group discussions. Several other responsibilities can be rotated, including refreshments, prayer requests, worship, or keeping up with those who miss a meeting. Shared ownership in the group helps everybody grow.

Where Do We Find New Group Members?

Recruiting new members can be challenging for groups, especially new groups with just a few people or existing groups that lose a few people along the way. We encourage you to use the **CIRCLES OF LIFE** diagram on page 132 of this study to brainstorm a list of people from your workplace, church, school, neighborhood, family, and so on. Then pray for the people on each member's list. Allow each member to invite several people from their list. Some groups fear that newcomers will interrupt the intimacy that members have built over time. However, groups that welcome newcomers generally gain strength with the infusion of new blood. Remember, the next person you add just might become a friend for eternity. Logistically, groups find different ways to add members. Some groups remain permanently open, while others open periodically, such as at the beginning or end of a study. If your group becomes too large for easy, face-to-face conversations, you can subgroup, forming a second discussion group in another room.

How Do We Handle the Child Care Needs In Our Group?

Childcare needs must be handled very carefully. This is a sensitive issue. We suggest you seek creative solutions as a group. One common solution is to have the adults meet in the living room and share the cost of a babysitter (or two) who can be with the kids in another part of the house. Another popular option is to have one supervised home for the kids and a second home (close by) for the adults. If desired, the adults could rotate the responsibility of providing a lesson for the kids. This last option is great with school-age kids and can be a huge blessing to families.

Small Group Guidelines

It's a good idea for every group to put words to their shared values, expectations, and commitments. Such guidelines will help you avoid unspoken agendas and unmet expectations. We recommend you discuss your guidelines during Week 1 in order to lay the foundation for a healthy group experience. Feel free to modify anything that does not work for your group. We agree to the following values:

CLEAR PURPOSE

Grow healthy spiritual lives by building a healthy small group community.

GROUP ATTENDANCE

Give priority to the group meeting (call or text if I am going to be absent or late).

SAFE ENVIRONMENT

Create a safe place where people can be heard and feel loved (no quick answers, snap judgments, or simple fixes).

BE CONFIDENTIAL

Keep anything that is shared strictly confidential and within the group.

CONFLICT RESOLUTION

Avoid gossip and immediately resolve any concerns by following the principles of Matthew 18:15–17.

SPIRITUAL HEALTH

Give group members permission to speak into my life and help me live a healthy, balanced spiritual life pleasing to God.

LIMIT OUR FREEDOM

Limit our freedom by not serving or consuming alcohol during small group meetings or events to avoid causing another brother or sister to stumble (1 Corinthians 8:9 NIV; Romans 14:21 NIV).

WELCOME NEWCOMERS

Invite friends who might benefit from this study and warmly welcome newcomers.

BUILD RELATIONSHIPS

Get to know the other members of the group and pray for them regularly.

OTHER

We have also discussed and agreed on the following items:

CHILD CARE

STARTING TIME

ENDING TIME

If you haven't already done so, take a few minutes to fill out the **SMALL GROUP CALENDAR** on page 134.

Circles of Life

Discover Who You Can Connect In Community

Use this Circles of Life diagram chart to help carry out one of the values in the **SMALL GROUP GUIDELINES**— to "Welcome Newcomers."

Follow this simple, three-step process: 1) List one to two people in each circle. 2) Prayerfully select one person or couple from your list, and tell your group about them. 3) Give them a call and invite them to your next meeting. Over 50 percent of those invited to a small group say, "Yes!"

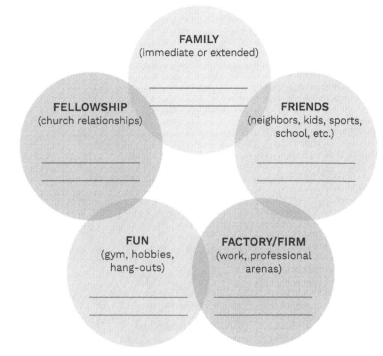

Prayer and Praise Report

This is a place where you can write each other's requests for prayer. You can also make a note when God answers a prayer. Pray for each other's requests. If you're new to group prayer, it's okay to pray silently or to pray by using just one sentence:

"God, please help _____ to _____."

DATE	PERSON	PRAYER REQUEST	PRAISE REPORT

Small Group Calendar

Healthy groups share responsibilities and group ownership. It might take some time for this to develop. Shared ownership ensures that responsibility for the group doesn't fall to one person. Use the calendar to keep track of social events, mission projects, birthdays, or days off. Complete this calendar at your first or second meeting. Planning ahead will increase attendance and shared ownership.

DATE	LESSON	LOCATION	FACILITATOR	SNACK OR MEAL
	Week 1			
	Week 2			
	Week 3			
	Week 4			
	Week 5			

Additional Resources*

The Five Purposes of Marriage

Marriage is one of the most
beautiful and complicated
ideas from God. The Bible talks
about two becoming one and
how it's not good for man to be
alone, but what is it about this
type of covenantal partnership that makes marriage
so unique? In *The Five Purposes of Marriage*, George
and Tondra Gregory answer the question, "Why Did
God Create Marriage?" and shed light on some of God's
purposes for bringing you and your spouse together.
This study, filled with practical tips and real-life
examples, will help you better understand the value
of marriage and appreciate your role in it. Available
at *sdbk.cc/marriagestudy*.

---

*Saddleback Church members can access these resources at
saddleback.com/studies.*

Spiritual Fitness Series

Sometimes, we need a good fitness regimen to stay in shape. This is true of our physical health, but it's also true of our spiritual health. Saddleback Church has released the first five volumes in its new Spiritual Fitness Series. These guidebooks will help you begin and maintain spiritual practices in your life.

Current titles in the series include:

- *Life of Prayer*
- *Memorizing Scripture*
- *Names of God*
- *Fasting and Prayer*
- *Daily Time in God's Word*

Available for purchase at: *sdbk.cc/fitness*

The Purpose, Practice, and Power of Prayer: Strategies for Spiritual Warfare

The Scripture makes it clear that we are in a great cosmic battle. It is not a battle against people. It is a battle against spiritual forces of evil that are trying to destroy the work  of God—in the world and in our lives. But God has equipped us, empowered us, authorized us, and called us to partner with him in accomplishing his purposes on Earth. And we do it primarily through prayer. This six-session, video-based study for small groups or individuals will help equip you to pray with greater purpose and power. Available at: *sdbk.cc/prayerstudy*

Small Group Roster

NAME	PHONE	EMAIL
1.		
2.		
3.		
4.		
5.		
6.		
7.		
8.		
9.		
10.		
11.		
12.		
13.		
14.		
15.		
16.		

Made in the USA
Las Vegas, NV
27 September 2023

78222063R00077